Door to Eternity

Irma Zaleski

NOVALIS

© 2001 Novalis, Saint Paul University, Ottawa, Canada
Cover: Blair Turner
Layout: Gilles Lépine
Business Office:
Novalis
49 Front Street East, 2nd Floor
Toronto, Ontario, Canada
M5E 1B3
Phone: 1-800-387-7164 or (416) 363-3303
Fax: 1-800-204-4140 or (416) 363-9409
E-mail: novalis@interlog.com

Canadian Cataloguing in Publication Data
Zaleski, Irma, 1931–
    Door to eternity
ISBN 2-89507-106-3
    1. Death–Religious aspects–Christianity. 2. Future life–
Christianity. I. Title.
BT825.Z35 2001   236'.1   C00901701-1

Printed in Canada.

We acknowledge the financial support of the Government of
Canada through the Book Publishing Industry Development
Program (BPIDP) for our publishing activities.

NOVALIS

Contents

Foreword

The subject of death has always fascinated me. Even as a child I tried to imagine what it would be like to die. I thought of it with fear, even with terror, but also with curiosity and excitement, with a kind of anxiety one would experience before a long journey to a strange and unknown destination. What fascinated me most deeply, I think, and still does, was the inevitability of it, the absolute certainty that one day, at one specific moment in time, it would be happening to *me,* that I too would be setting out on that journey. Nothing in life, nothing at all, could be as certain, as inevitable as death.

The reality of death was not a difficult idea to arrive at for me and for countless children of my generation growing up in Europe. I was only eight years old when the Second World War began. During the next seven years, we lived surrounded by death: death among family and friends; death from torture and beatings, from firing squads and bombs; death on the street, in prisons, in ghettos and concentration camps. After the war, as we tried to rebuild our lives in a new country and, eventually, on the new continent, the sense of ever-present death receded, but it never quite left me; it lay like an edge of darkness around everything I did and thought and believed in. How could it be otherwise? I *knew* that death was real.

Now, of course, as I grow old, the reality of death is again ever more present to me. There are times when death – my own death – seems just a step away, on the other side of the lake at which I live, or perhaps behind the next line of trees, over the next hill. Sometimes I feel that I am already in the waiting room and, before too long, the door will open and I shall have to go through it. But because I cannot understand or imagine what it will be like, what kind of reality awaits me on the other side, what will become of *me,* I – like every other human being who has ever lived – am assailed by fear.

It is the uncertainty – the *unknowing,* I have come to realize, that is the cause of our greatest fear. Our minds cannot cope with what is beyond their ability to grasp and to control. There can be no science or technology that would make our dying easy and its outcome assured. The only certainty we can have, the only sure hope, is the certainty of faith: of our trust not in ourselves, but in God. But such faith and trust are very difficult for most of us to find and even more difficult to hold onto when we begin to face the mystery of our own inevitable end.

And yet, as I look back on my own life, it seems to me that however difficult and convoluted my own path of faith has been and still is, however tormented by fear and doubt, it has led me, in the end, to a place of great hope. The mystery of death points to a possibility of joy and glory so immense, so exciting and so infinitely beyond anything we can ever dream of or imagine, that it is worth giving up our life for it. And we give it up – we die – not only once, at the end of our earthly existence, but at every moment of our lives. This is our *daily death* and daily resurrection. It is also our life's work. This, at least, is what I have come to believe.

Irma Zaleski

The Gap of Death

For most of us, death is not a part of our everyday reality. If we think of it at all, we think of it only as a future event, something that happens to us at one precise moment in time, at the end of our earthly lives. The country of death does not exist for us until we arrive at its door. In a very real way, this is, clearly, true. The moment of death is a unique, unavoidable moment in the future, a final step in our journey on earth. It is the end of our physical existence, of everything that is familiar to us, everything that is accessible to our minds. It is, as it were, a "gap" of mysterious and unknowable darkness that divides our life on earth from eternity and which we all must, one day, enter, never to return again.

This mysterious, unknowable gap, this "place" of our dying, is not, of course, a place in any physical sense, and our entry into it is not an event in time as we understand it on earth. It is rather a *level of reality* that we all have to enter and to pass through on the way to eternity. This entering and passing are our inevitable future, but also – and this is very important for us to realize – an inseparable part of our daily existence.

Death is not only one specific instant at the end of life, but exists and calls to us in every moment of our earthly life. We have to *live* death. It is this lived death – our *daily death* – to which Christ called us when he said that if we want to be his disciples, we must *deny ourselves* and *lose our life.* (Mark 8:34–35) To deny oneself, to lose one's life, is to embrace the cross of our daily dying. The two deaths are not two but one – they are two sides of the same coin, two arms of the same cross, they can never be separated.

We *die daily*, not only because with each moment we approach the end of our earthly existence, but also because each moment we must (for we have no choice) let go of everything that has been, all our past, and face a new, unknown reality, a new beginning of time. Everything around us – nature, the rhythm of our own bodies, each breath we take, our fleeting thoughts – tells us that it is so. *To bear fruit, to give life, the seed must fall into the ground and die.* (John 12:24)

To bear fruit and grow into the fullness of life to which we have been called, we must let our poor earthly selves die – must surrender our lives – not just once, but every day of our lives. It is only by embracing our "daily death" that we can, while still on earth, cross the gap and *begin* our entrance into eternity, which lies *beyond* death, and have a glimpse of its glory. Death, in this life or the next, is our *door into eternity*; there is no other.

Eternity

In the same way as we tend to view death as a future event, we tend to view eternity as "afterlife" and imagine it as an endless progression of time that begins for us at the moment of death. But eternity lies *beyond* the dimension of time, and the categories we use in describing our earthly reality do not apply to it. There is no past or future in eternity as we know them on earth. Eternity is timeless – it always *is* and thus it is always *present* to us. It encompasses and penetrates every moment of our earthly time. In a very real sense, we already *are* in eternity, we *live* in it.

When we say that eternity "lies beyond the dimension of time," we do not mean that it is a different kind of time, yet another dimension of earthly reality that may – if not now, then sometime in the future – be discovered and understood by the human mind, that can be studied and eventually measured by science. Eternity, in the way in which religion understands it, is not a physical but a spiritual reality; it is participation in the eternal *now* of God. Like all spiritual realities, it is beyond the capacity of the human mind to discover or "prove," however advanced our science and technology might become.[1]

In the Christian Tradition, the word "eternity"

has two related but distinct meanings. First of all, it means *immortality* – life without end – which has been granted to each one of us when, at the moment of our conception, God breathed his spirit into us and thus "clothed" our mortality with immortality. Second, it signifies *eternal life,* which is eternity spent in the presence of and in union with God, who has always been, who is, and will be forever, without end.

It is because we are *spiritual beings* – we have souls as well as bodies – that we cannot truly die. All of us, good or bad, have immortal souls. Our bodies, or at least as we know them on earth, like the whole of physical creation, are subject to death and dissolution, but our souls – the *spiritual principle* in us – cannot be dissolved.[2] They may be transformed, sanctified or, God forbid, depraved, but they cannot be destroyed. No power on earth – not even the devil himself – can really kill us.

It is in that sense that we can say that death does not exist, that it is a myth and an illusion we must give up. Killing others or killing ourselves – any kind of attempt to solve our problems through death – is not only a terrible evil and sin but also, in the words of a wonderful Zen saying, as futile as "cutting water with a knife." Immortality has been given to us by God; only he could take it away from us, and this he will never do. God does not break his promises or revoke his gifts. We "survive death"[3] and live forever in eternity whether we want to or not.

12

Eternal Life

When we say that we believe in *eternal life*, however, we mean something much more than that we believe in the immortality of the soul. To have eternal life means to share in the divine life of God, to live forever in his presence, to be *one with him* now, in this life, and after death.

Although the way to eternal life (i.e., eternity spent in union with God) is open to all, it is not granted "automatically" to us. It is not thrust upon us whether we want it or not. Its "seed" – the divine image in which we were created – has been planted in each human being coming into the world. Yet, in order for the seed to grow to its full potential, we must embrace it through faith and live it through love. We *can* refuse to believe it, and live as if it did not exist. It is this state of denial and refusal – if we persist in it to the end – that we call "eternal death." It is not the end of the soul, because the soul can have no end, but its total, awful *defeat*.

We choose our eternal destiny every moment of our earthly time. Whatever we do, our every word or thought, every breath we take, is already immersed in eternity and has an eternal significance. While we are still on earth, we exist in the progression of time. We live moment by moment. But as spiritual beings we can already, if we so choose, participate in the "no-time" – the eternal *present* – of eternity.

Belief in the possibility of coexistence of time and eternity lies at the root of all religion. Religion can be even, perhaps, defined as a path, or a "ladder" to such a coexistence. Christian teaching makes the truth of this belief absolutely clear. The creed, the liturgy, the sacraments, the icons, proclaim it: Christ, a man like us, born at a precise moment of history, living in a small corner of the Roman Empire, dying on the hill of Calvary, buried and risen on the third day, and Christ the Eternal Word, coexistent with the Father. Christ with us now, on earth, and Christ already ascended into heaven, sitting in glory at the right hand of the Father. Christ *the Alpha and the Omega*, the Beginning and the End, in whom time and eternity meet.

And so it is with us. We are here, at this specific moment of our lives, still bowed down under the burden of our mortality, but the hour of our passing is already known and *present* to God, who is beyond time. We are already immersed in his glory and light. We have been "baptized into Christ's death" and are buried with him, but we have also already risen with him and are with him in eternity, at home. This is the great mystery of faith, the reality of the eternal *presence* of God "in whom we live and move and have our being." (Acts 17:28) Yet, because we cannot *know* it – because we cannot grasp it with our finite, human minds or see it with our earthly eyes – it appears to us as darkness and we are afraid.

The Fear of Death

Most of us await death with fear, even with terror, some with cynicism or resignation, some with despair or rage. The thought of our own dying fills us with dread, and we struggle, sometimes for most of our lives, to suppress or deny it, even to ourselves. The denial of death is so common in our society that its opposite – awareness of death, willingness to face it and to accept it – is often considered morbid and uncivilized.

Even when the unthinkable happens and death does take place, we talk about it in whispers and refer to it in euphemisms: our dead are not dead but have "passed away"; our funeral establishments are "homes" or "parlours" where we visit our "departed" relatives or friends. We impose awful indignities on their bodies to make them appear alive so that we are not forced to face the reality of their dissolution. Our funerals are as short as we can make them; we rush away from the cemetery leaving the casket hidden under its blanket of flowers, and the earth, which is to cover it, under a carpet of artificial grass.

What is it about death that makes us so afraid? Partly, of course, it is our natural apprehension about what may happen to us *before* death. We are afraid of the sickness, physical pain and loss of control that often precede death. No rational person can avoid thinking and worrying about this at times, especially when old age is upon us and the body begins to send signals that the dissolution has begun.

We also dread having to leave behind everybody and everything we care for. We agonize that those who love us and depend on us may have to struggle on alone. We anticipate their sorrow and their sense of loss: we grieve *with* them. As Dr. Kübler-Ross has shown us, we *mourn* our own death.[4]

The greatest fear that haunts us, however, is, it seems to me, the fear of dying itself. We are afraid of that final moment in time, a split second, perhaps, when we come to the very end of life and must inevitably, irrevocably, pass on; when the body remains, but life, *our life*, must leave it behind; when we find ourselves face to face with a reality about which we ourselves know nothing and nobody living can tell us.

There is no one answer to our fear of death. All of us must come to terms with it in the way that is most true – most real – to us. The stark reality of our end accepts no self-delusion or pretense. The moment of death must surely be the moment of ultimate truth about who we truly are and what we truly believe. This may well be a very frightening possibility for us. Perhaps we have already begun to suspect how puny we truly are and how little we truly believe: how unprepared we are for what we now must face and how uncertain we are of its outcome.

Dread of the Unknown

Because our minds cannot throw any light on what awaits us on the other side of the door of death, we are terrified at what we shall find. Because we cannot know or imagine what "self" may be left to us after our body disintegrates, we are always tempted to expect total annihilation. The fear of death, the dreadful, gnawing terror which at times touches us all, is, I think, above all, the fear of darkness, of the *unknown*.

We dread not-knowing, because it makes us feel powerless. Always we strive to achieve power to control our own lives and believe that only knowledge – rational knowledge – can give it to us. We equate not-knowing with ignorance and irrationality, a dangerous, destructive power that can play havoc with our lives. And so we struggle to build places of safety for ourselves, we surround ourselves with walls, we plan and try to arrange our future so we can always know what to expect. We cling to the illusion that we can control what happens to us even a moment from now.

How very difficult, then, it must be for us to realize that we have no power at all over what happens to us at the most terrifying moment of our lives, the moment we cannot escape! We cannot bear the thought of entering the gap of death alone, in the dark, unable to know what to expect. We cannot accept the fact that such knowledge is unavailable to us.

Sometimes, we search for it in strange places. We avidly grasp at every vision, every revelation or mystical experience we might hear about. We travel to distant places and embrace unfamiliar spiritual paths. We try to communicate with the dead, or pray for signs or "significant" dreams, for anything that will enable us to glimpse the reality beyond. Yet, in the end, after we have, perhaps, exhausted ourselves on this search, after we have spent years and much of our spiritual energy on it, do we really know any more than we had known before, or understand any more fully what awaits us at death? Have we really "solved" the mystery of death?

It is true, we may have many consoling – or terrifying – images and ideas floating around in our minds, but what good will they do us when we finally arrive at the gate of eternity, when our hearts have stopped, our brains are silent and there is not one idea or image left to us? When we are summoned to a meeting with God whose mind we cannot ever know but who sees every movement of our heart and soul? When, willing or unwilling, ready or not, we have to begin the journey into the unknown darkness we have feared all our lives?

Attempts to Peer
Across the Gap

It is often assumed that people with strong religious beliefs should be able to face the moment of death without dread; that, for them, the way across is revealed and clearly marked; that they are told in their sacred scriptures and teachings what they must expect to find on the other side, what dangers they must face and how they can avoid them. This may be true of some religions, but it is, perhaps surprisingly, not true in the case of Christianity.

Christians are not given any secret or "esoteric" knowledge of the mystery of death or granted any immunity from fear. There is no Christian "Book of the Dead." We are not handed a detailed "guide-book" of dying or any instructions for safely crossing the gap. Like the whole of humanity, like Christ himself, we too, when our "hour" arrives, must go into the darkness of not-knowing relying on nothing but God.

It is true that a few of the early saints and teachers of the Christian Tradition (whom we usually call "the Fathers") have written in some detail about what they believed happened to a soul at the moment of death and during the difficult passage to the other side. They warned about many great dangers and trials which a soul would encounter and about difficult "tests" it would have to pass. They derived their teachings from the insights, dreams and "death experiences" of some saints.[5]

Nothing that the saints have said or done can be without value to our life of faith. We should not, therefore, dismiss their insights too readily and without thought. On the other hand, these insights should not be taken literally, for they are not meant to offer us scientific information or instruct us in celestial geography. Some of the images used by the Fathers were clearly based on an understanding of physical reality which can no longer be maintained. Some, perhaps, are a reflection of general, not necessarily Christian, beliefs about afterlife prevalent during the time they lived. It can be said, I think, that these images, like all religious images, should encourage us to contemplate the "heavenly reality" they seek to represent, but not to imagine that they describe it as it really is.

Most of these writings and images were produced in the Christian East, and are practically unknown in the West. Western Christians, however, have not been free from speculation about what happens at death. There have been many reports of "private revelations" and visions of death and afterlife. Art and literature, as well as popular piety and imagination, especially in the Middle Ages, have loved to dwell on every possible imagined scenario of dying, judgment and, above all, on the horrifying torments of hell. These images became so popular and so firmly entrenched in people's minds and imaginations that for many they have become "gospel truth." Even now – for better or for worse – they continue to play a significant part in the religious life of many Christians.

It is important to remember, however, that these various attempts to "peer beyond the gap," both in the East and in the West, are not part of the universal teaching of the Christian Church. They do not belong to what Catholic theology calls "the deposit of faith," the essential "message" given to the apostles by Christ and entrusted by them to the whole Church. They are products of human imagination and piety. We should therefore show great care and discrimination in how we receive them and how we try to pass them on to others. We must not add any "frills" to what has been handed down to us, or let ourselves be misled through "any empty, seductive philosophy that follows mere human traditions not based on Christ." (Colossians 2:8)

The same caution should be exercised in connection with many recent reports and studies of "life after life" experiences of people who had undergone clinical death but were later revived. Although these accounts may be helpful and reassuring, even inspiring, to many, we should not forget that they only attempt to describe what happens *before* the actual and irreversible death has taken place. Thus, they are still experiences of *this* life. They cannot, therefore, offer any reliable evidence about what actually happens to us at the moment of death or, most importantly, about our entrance into afterlife. That remains the mystery which, it seems, God has meant it to be.

Mystery
of the World to Come

It was surely not an oversight – an inadvertent omission – on the part of Christ to have told us so little about the reality that awaits us after death. Although he spoke often of the need to await our death with watchfulness and warned us of the judgment we must face, he did not "describe" afterlife, and when he referred to it at all he spoke in parables and metaphors. He did not say a word about what it was like to lie in the tomb, to visit the dead in the place of darkness and then to rise again. He did not find it necessary to tell us what he "saw." This may be disappointing and surprising at first, but could he have done otherwise?

If it were possible to explain and express in human words life after death, surely it would mean that eternity was still *finite* – within the human mind's limited ability to know and comprehend. In other words, it would be of the same order of reality as our present life. This kind of "eternity" could never satisfy us. Would we really want to live this earthly life forever, however happy and free from suffering we might imagine it to be? Would we not get bored with it, as we seem to get bored with everything in life? Would we be willing to give up everything we have – even our life – to gain such an ordinary prize?

If we struggle to overcome our limitations in this life and accept the call for self-denial, if we strain after holiness and long for God, it is because, in our heart of hearts, we realize that we have been created for a bigger and more glorious life. As St. Paul reminds us, what awaits us after death is beyond anything that "the eye has seen or the ear has heard," and *beyond anything the mind of man can grasp*. (1 Corinthians 2:9) Mother Maria Gysi expressed it this way:

> We have to bend under the not-knowing because we do not know what immensities open up after death. What we are preparing for is bigger and of a different order, of wholly different standards and values, from that which we know now.[6]

We encounter this thought from the very beginnings of the Church. Already St. John insisted that, while still on earth, it was not possible for us to know or speak about the reality of life after death. We are already the children of God and live in his presence, but what we shall become in the life to come has not yet been revealed. (1 John 3:2) As Bishop Kallistos Ware wrote in his *Orthodox Way,*

Through our faith in Christ, we possess here and now a living, personal relationship with God, and we know, not as a hypothesis, but as a present fact of experience, that this relationship already contains within itself the seeds of eternity. But, what it is to live not within the time sequence but in the eternal Now ... in a universe where God is 'all in all' – of this we have only partial glimpses but no clear conception; and so we should speak always with caution, respecting the need for silence.[7]

We should not be too hasty to speak about things which we cannot know and which cannot really be expressed in words. We should not grudge God his mysteries, for they are signs of the inexpressible glory that is our end and our true home. The mystery of death and our inability to penetrate it with our finite minds reminds us always of the Infinite Reality – the "immensities" – which surround and await us all. There is a world beyond our ordinary world, the world revealed to us only by faith.

Faith

When we say that we cannot *know* what happens to us at death or comprehend the eternity that awaits us, we do not mean to say that no light has been given to us to penetrate the darkness beyond our earthly existence. But this light is not the light of reason but of *faith*.

Most contemporary Christians, especially in the West, do not understand the true nature of faith. We are too often unaware of the immense beauty and power of the divine light that shines within our own souls. For most of us, faith is but a flickering light. We tend to view it as a lesser kind of knowledge than that which can be gained by our rational, thinking minds, which we generally consider to be the highest gift given to the human race. But faith is not a smaller gift than thought; rather, it is immeasurably greater. Faith is a spiritual gift given to the soul, and, like the soul, it is stronger than death. All our ideas and images must leave us at death; our thinking – at least as we understand it on earth – stops with our brains, but the light of faith remains with us and guides us across the gap of death until we are safely through, in that eternal reality beyond all knowledge, which God has prepared for those who love him. (1 Corinthians 9)

The gift of faith, in the Christian Tradition, is a gift of humble *assent* to the invisible reality of "heavenly things" revealed by God in Christ. St. Thomas Aquinas called faith "an act of the intellect assenting to the divine truth."[8] In other words, our minds cannot discover or judge the truth of faith, they can only assent to it when it is presented to them. For this reason, in Catholic theology, the assent of faith is often understood as an "act of the will." It is our will which moves our reason to belief. We *choose* to believe.

It is important, however, not to interpret belief as only, or mainly, a matter of intellect and will. Faith is not a passive acceptance of some "definitions" or "formulas" pronounced by an authority we must obey,[9] but rather an inner recognition that what is being taught to us is the very truth that has been planted in our own soul, and which we can already, however "darkly – as in a mirror," experience. (1 Corinthians 13:12) It is the same experience as that of the two disciples on the road to Emmaus, whose hearts "burned" within them when Christ spoke to them, although they did not know yet who he was.

Faith is above all a matter of *love*. It is, as the Orthodox Church ceaselessly reminds us, an assent given in the heart – not our physical heart but the inner "core," the very centre of our being. It is a vision of the heart. Faith "happens" when we "see" – recognize – a truth in our heart and embrace it freely in love. It is what Catherine Doherty, the foundress of Madonna House, called "falling in love with God."[10] Faith pierces our hearts and opens them to hope, wonder and joy. As the great Greek Father of the Church, St. Basil, wrote in the fourth century,

> When we contemplate the blessings of faith even now, as if gazing at a reflection in a mirror, it is as if we already possessed the wonderful things which our faith assures us we shall one day enjoy.[11]

To believe in the "wonderful things" which God has prepared for us in eternity means to believe that they are true not only in some general way – like a historical fact, for instance – but true for *us,* that they are a present reality to us, that they become, as it were, the form and pattern of our own being. And, above all, it means to be "assured" that God is present to us *now,* that we can recognize him when he appears before the eyes of our hearts – when he reveals himself to us and that we can love him and are willing to trust him, blindly, even when we cannot see him, when we feel abandoned and totally alone.

Trust in God

To trust God "blindly" means to trust him without asking for any "proof" or explanations, any guarantees in life or death. It means to abandon oneself totally into his hands and *believe* in his infinite goodness and mercy, whatever life – or death – might bring to us. It means to believe that God's will for us is that we should possess the fullness of life for which he created us; that he cannot ever will our destruction or condemnation in this life or the next. Our living and dying are safe in his hands.

This does not mean, of course, that, as we approach our inevitable end, we are free of all fear or doubt and dance with joy at the prospect of death! Such an extraordinary faith and trust is granted to a few saints, but is given to most of us. We should not complain, however, for the price of such a gift may be beyond our ability to pay. It requires a total surrender: the death of self, willingness to abdicate every "right" we might think we have, even of our right to heaven![12] Few of us are willing or able to pay such a price. And even those who do, the greatest of saints, those who have loved God and trusted him the most, may find that their fear does not leave them at the end; that they may be asked to trust in

31

spite of their fear. St. Thérèse herself, after a life spent in a childlike trust in God, could still write these words, shortly before her death:

> I am afraid I have feared death. I am not afraid of what happens after death; that is certain! I don't regret giving up my life; but I ask myself: What is this mysterious separation of the soul from the body? It is the first time that I have experienced this, but I *abandoned myself immediately to God*.[13]

We should not expect greater courage of ourselves! We, too, when we realize how afraid we are, should not lose heart but "abandon ourselves immediately to God." We should ask him ceaselessly to increase our trust so that, when the hour of our death arrives, we may meet it, if not without fear, at least with a little courage and a measure of peace. We should remind ourselves that our dying will not be for us a leap of terror, but a leap of faith – our final meeting with the infinite mercy and love of God. This is, perhaps, the only "knowledge" of death we need to possess and the source of all our hope.

Christian Hope

Christian hope of eternal life – our "living hope," as St. Peter calls it – is based on faith in the resurrection of Jesus Christ from the dead. (1 Peter 1:3) Christ has not demolished physical death – for we all must die – but, by his own undeserved, "voluntary" death he has "taken away its sting"; he has "trampled death by death," as the Easter Liturgy of St. John Chrysostom ceaselessly proclaims. If Christ had not risen, St. Paul says, all our hope would be in vain and we could have no assurance of eternal life at all. (1 Corinthians 15:14) The light that shines across the gap of death is the light of the risen Lord.

Viewed in the light of the presence of the risen Christ, death can never be considered a merely "natural" event – an unavoidable end of our earthly life. Death is also, always, a spiritual reality, perhaps the most spiritually powerful event of our lives. For it is possible, I think, to say that Christian death is sacramental; that, like all sacraments, it is a sign and pledge of eternal life and a source of grace. At the moment of death, if we open ourselves, however poorly, to the divine presence coming to meet us, if we can surrender ourselves to it and embrace it, it will fill us with its own life and raise us again by the power of its love. In the words of St. Maximus the Confessor, each death is an "initiation into the mystery of the resurrection."[14]

It is sometimes difficult for us to understand how the resurrection of Christ, an event that happened all those centuries ago, can be so relevant to our own present spiritual life. We experience a longing for holiness and fullness of life *now,* in this life, not only in eternity. We feel, perhaps rightly, that we are not yet fully alive, that we are, as it were, in a tomb, and we do not see how the fact of Christ's resurrection can change that. Is Christian hope to be fulfilled in the future, perhaps at the moment of death, or even at the Last Judgment, or does it have any significance for our lives now?

We often go through life convinced that we "believe" in God, in Christ, in all the "truths" of our religion, without ever realizing that these truths are not only truths about Christ but also, fundamentally, truths about ourselves. Each mystery of Christ's life on earth, as well as of his death, must be reproduced in us. Christ has to be *incarnated* and born in us, we must live his life of surrender and love and we must die with him, in order to rise with him and ascend with him to heaven. The "spirit of Christ" is to be our spirit too. Unless we "empty ourselves" as he did (Philippians 2:7) and allow this spirit to fill us, we cannot have the fullness of eternal life either here on earth or in heaven.

To understand this truth is so essential to our life of faith that it must be repeated over and over again, until it penetrates into the depth of our being and wakes us up to its full significance. Our hope of eternal life lies in our willingness to allow ourselves to die, so that we might open ourselves to the new life manifested to us in Jesus, and become transformed into another Christ.

Divinization

The Eastern Christian Fathers referred to this process as *theosis*, which in Greek means *divinization* or "deification": transformation of a human person so profound, so total, that it allows us to apply to him or her the words of St. Paul when he said, "I live, and yet not I but Christ who lives in me." (Galatians 2:20) To have eternal life is to *lose* the life we are now living and to live – literally – the divine life of Christ.

This concept appears so amazing to most contemporary Christians, at least in the West, so "daring," that they find it nearly impossible to believe that it really is part of the ancient teaching of the Church. And yet, it is so. Divinization is the final goal – one might say the logical conclusion – of the Incarnation of God in Christ. Christ became man in order that we could become "sharers in the divine nature" (2 Peter 1:2) or, as St. Athanasius wrote in the fourth century, "God became man, that man could become God." (De Inc. 54) And St. Basil is reported to have said that "man is a creature who received the command to become God."[14]

To become divinized, in the language of the Fathers, means to become another Christ, to become one with the incarnated Man-God.

Through his life, death and resurrection, the divine energy – the Holy Spirit – has been poured out on the world. Its work is to transform all things into what they have been created to be. When we are divinized, we "become by grace what Christ was by nature"[16] and reach the final end for which we were created.

But how can this be? We are, or appear to be, in a state of such profound ignorance, indifference and confusion, so unaware of who we are and what we are called to be, that the hope of such a transformation may seem foolish indeed. This apparent inability or unwillingness of Christians to live the life of Christ has been a scandal and a "stumbling block" from the beginning. St. Paul acknowledged it; the early Fathers struggled to understand it and wept over it.

They came to see it as an inherited weakness of all humanity and a result of some terrible failure of mind and will, of a radically wrong choice on the part of our first parents that they called "the Fall." They saw us as exiles from our own true nature, fallen from the dignity we were meant to have and "banished" from Paradise. Yet they also believed that the original purpose of God to bring us to the fullness of life has not been and can never be totally frustrated; that God "became flesh" to show us the path of life and to open to us, again, the way to Paradise. This is the goal of *theosis*.

The Way of Surrender

The need for transformation has been taught by every religious tradition and spiritual path. It has been generally recognized that transformation cannot be reached by human efforts alone, but is the work of the divine life and energy which fills the universe and manifests itself in our own hearts, and to which we must learn to *surrender*. It is this learning to surrender — to open ourselves to the divine work in us — which is the goal of every true spiritual practice.

What is unique in Christianity, however, is the conviction that Christ, as the perfect manifestation — the incarnation — of the divine life and power, is more than a great model of a fully divinized being. Christ is not only a great — or even the greatest — teacher pointing out the path of transformation, but he *is* the path and its goal. The Christian path of transformation is the process of being transformed into Christ. It is always understood as participation in the divine life of Christ.

This process is never viewed as "spiritualization" of life, as a kind of "transmutation" of matter into spirit, as it seems to be viewed in some non-Christian religions. It is not, strictly speaking, understood as a process of *ascent* (this image often appears in Christian spiritual writing) of a human person into a state of "higher consciousness," or of a purely spiritual mode of existence, but as *descent* of the Divine into the human reality. It is the same work of the Holy Spirit that worked in Mary to bring about the Incarnation of the Son of God in her womb and that will also work in us, if we too open ourselves to it. Divinization does not discard our humanity but completes and fulfills it. It makes us – body, soul and spirit – into a "temple" of the Holy Spirit, a "sacrament" of the divine life and presence. This point is fundamental to the Christian understanding of eternal life, of love, of holiness, as well as of the sacraments, the liturgy and of the whole life of the Church. Every aspect of Christian teaching loses its true significance if we forget that a human being is not composed of "parts," but is one indivisible person.

At the same time, this insistence on the unity of our being does not mean to deny that within that one indivisible person there might exist different levels of reality. A human being might be viewed as one indivisible *continuum*. The Scriptures and the Fathers often seem to suggest that our spirit is, in fact, the "highest" principle in that continuum. It is highest because it is "closest" to the spiritual world, to the divine reality. It reflects God most clearly of all. But it is not to be understood as separable from the whole.

Human spirit is a channel through which the Holy Spirit flows "down" the continuum and gives life to it all. Or, to use another image, it is a spark that lights our whole being with the fire of the divine life.

Belief in divinization proclaims, I think, in a most profound way, the original greatness and beauty of the human person as created by God. In the face of evil, disaster and sin, it insists on the possibility of rebirth, of restoration of this greatness and beauty and offers a hope of fulfillment and glory so immense, and so unexpected, that it is hard for most of us even to begin to believe that we too have been called to it. It is a treasure, the Good News, too often forgotten, too often dimmed by our inability to live it out. Nevertheless, it is a treasure that Christianity can offer to the world.

Conversion

Western Christians, although they have always shared the belief in the need and promise of transformation, did not, on the whole, use the term "divinization" for it. Perhaps it was felt that the idea of divinization did not make the truth of the transcendence of God clear enough, or that it might mislead some into thinking that human beings could ever assume the infinite *nature* and power of God. Western theologians preferred to talk about the transformation of the individual *soul* through the "indwelling" of the Holy Trinity in it, and through Man-God Christ "abiding" in it and uniting himself with it through love. (John 14:23)

But whether we think of the way of transformation as divinization, or, perhaps less boldly, as a way of union of the soul with God incarnated in Christ, the "work" of transformation is always seen as the work of God's grace "turning us around" and calling us to a radical re-direction of our whole lives. Our part in this work, as has been said already, and our main task as disciples of Christ, is to surrender to the grace and cooperate with it. This process of surrender and cooperation the Greek Fathers called *metanoia:* conversion of mind and heart.

41

When we enter the way of conversion we renounce self-love, in order to have more life and a greater love. Self-love is the way we focus on ourselves to the exclusion of all else, in which we protect ourselves against any possible hurt or harm from "outside": from our neighbour, from the world. and even sometimes from God. Self-love does not only mean protecting our own physical well-being, our health, our wealth or our security. We can also cling to our intelligence or knowledge, our piety, our "righteousness," and use them to defend ourselves from others, to belittle or manipulate them. This is a very dangerous form of self-love, difficult to recognize in ourselves, and very difficult to give up.

The process of conversion is sometimes explained by St. Augustine's concept of "two loves." We can, and must, make a choice between two desires, two goals in life. We either choose self-love (we choose to serve primarily ourselves, to place our good above the good of others) or we choose to "deny ourselves" (to put our own interests aside, to love and serve others and, above all, to love and serve God). When we choose God first and no longer consider ourselves the centre of the universe, we are "turned around." We lose our self-centredness and thus we become capable of love.

We must not imagine that conversion is an instant miracle. It is the *goal* of life, but it does not happen all at once. It remains a *process* – slow and painful at times – that we must be willing to undergo. It is a way of carrying the daily cross of our humanity, of bearing the burden of our seemingly inexhaustible self-love: the way of falling and rising, again and again. Conversion is the way of returning to God, the source of our life, not once, not seven times, but seventy times seven every day. It is a way of "losing our life" and dying to self every moment of our lives.

Dying to Self

The expression "dying to self" is often used, and its meaning seems quite clear. We assume it to be an evident truth that we do have a "self" or perhaps even two "selves." There is, we suppose, a mysterious, inner part of ourselves – "our true self" – which defines us as individual human beings, but which most of us have still to discover. This true self is usually identified with awareness, with "higher consciousness," with the soul, the mind, or the spiritual principle in us.

On the other hand, it is believed, we have a "false" self – a small, frightened, compulsive, unaware self, acquired by most of us through many negative experiences in life. It is this "self" that suffers from the illusion of being "special," being separate, and is terrified of dissolution and death. From this perspective, "dying to self" will mean finding our true self and getting rid of the false one. A search for our "true self," for "raising our consciousness," for overcoming the illusion of our small, separate self, seems to many of us – including many Christians – to be the greatest task of life. Modern psychology, as well as much religious writing, also seems to suggest it.

It may surprise us to learn that such a concept of self was not known to the writers of the New Testament, or to the early Fathers of the Church. Both in the Scriptures and in early Christian literature, the word "self" was used solely as a reflexive pronoun referring to the human individual as a whole. It was used in the same sense as the Hebrew Bible uses it when it commands us to "love our neighbour as we love ourselves" or, indeed, as we use it in everyday phrases such as "to hurt oneself," "to please oneself," "to feed oneself," and so on.

This is important to realize, because to think of "self" as a separate, "exchangeable" part of an individual, or even as the only truly significant part, distorts the fundamental belief of the biblical tradition in the unity of each human person about which we have talked above. In both Judaic and Christian religious thought, we are complex and often confused beings; we may sometimes feel as if there were different separate "selves" or "parts" within us fighting each other; we may have different and conflicting self-images but in reality we only have, or rather, we *are* inseparably one being: one self. Our "self" means simply *ourselves*: our whole, unique, individual life.

Thus, whenever we talk of our "dying to self," or even of the "death of self," it is important to remember that we do not mean a death, or a denial of a part of ourselves. Rather, we mean the same process of conversion about which we have spoken above: a complete turning away from self-love and a daily surrender of our whole being to God. It is the same process to which Christ called us when he said that, if we want to follow him – to live *his* life – we must "take up our daily cross, deny ourselves (he himself never used the expression 'to die to self') and lose our life. (Mark 8:34-37) He meant a change in ourselves – in our whole life – so fundamental and at times so painful that it is in fact a *death*.[17]

This process of "dying" is never perfectly completed on earth. For some of us, it may seem that it has hardly even begun! Perhaps, after a lifetime of trying, we still find ourselves hardly changed at all. We "lapse," we fail, we very often sin. The choice "for God" has to be made again and again. To realize this is not to indulge in neurotic guilt, but to face the reality of who we are before God. Which one of us would dare to claim that we are already "another Christ"? That we never lose our way? That we are "completed," perfect, as "our heavenly Father is perfect"? That we are ready to meet him face to face?

God's Work in Us

Realization of our weakness and inability to remain always faithful to the gift of life that God has lavished upon us should not lead us to discouragement or despair. We do not transform ourselves, but God does it in us. Christ is the vine; we are the branches grafted onto him. His divine life in which we must share – which we must *become* – is beyond time and space and cannot be diminished or destroyed by anything we do. It is a treasure kept safe for us in heaven. (Matthew 6:19) We can, of course, deny or reject the gift and turn away from the source, but as soon as we re-turn and open ourselves to it again – at every moment of our lives and, especially, at the moment of death – it fills us again and transforms us with its power and light. We become Christ again.

It may be said that the divine life of Christ is like the sun shining down on us from an immense, clear sky, ceaselessly pouring its light on us. But if clouds of self-centredness or sin should obscure the view, we are left "heavenless," in shadow of darkness and in fear. As soon, however, as we "come to ourselves" (as the prodigal son did in that parable of Jesus) and wake up from our self-absorption or pride, the clouds dissolve, we are freed from darkness and again enclosed by light.

It is this profound insight into the nature of the process of transformation that is the source of the Christian belief that eternal life – heaven – can be gained even at the end of our lives, even at the very moment of entering eternity, regardless of the lives we have led, or how grievously we have sinned. This truth is often difficult for us to accept. Such a "happy ending" may seem to us unjust – even scandalous – as it seemed to the "good" brother of the prodigal son, or to the tired labourers of another parable who had worked all day in the heat of the vineyard, but still received the same wage as those who came last.

The point of the two parables, however, is not to show us that scandalous life, or idleness, are just as good as goodness and hard work. The point is the same as the one made above: that fullness of life – of transformation – is the work of God. The party to end all parties takes place only when we surrender ourselves to the goodness and generosity of God. Whenever we turn away from it (and who does not, at times), when we want to "achieve" perfection on our own, when we think we have "deserved" it – we become, like the older brother, imprisoned in ourselves and resentful of the mercy shown to others. Yet what of those of us who may not have been so good, who may have dissipated all the wealth bestowed on us by God? As soon as we "come to our senses," as soon as we repent and throw ourselves on the mercy of God, we are restored to our inheritance and clothed in the "garments of salvation" that have been kept safe for us.

Expansion of Life

We are, then, beginning to see that what we call death and what we call life are two aspects of the same reality. Death is simply an expansion of life. Our dying is a way for us to break out of the bounds of our own small "selves," to "lose our life," and to be "extended" into the infinity of Christ's life. It is this constant movement of life into death, and death into life, that is the way we "pass over" and enter eternity every day of our earthly life.

Here, perhaps, an important point should be made. When we talk about dying – our daily dying, or our dying at the end – as a "passage into eternity" or as an "expansion of life," we are talking from the perspective of faith. We do not mean to deny the fact that death can be, and often is, a terrifying and incredibly painful experience, or that it can appear senseless and unjust. Some deaths are unspeakably horrible: mass killings of war, genocide, murder, the death of a child, a painful terminal illness. To deny their horror or attempt to offer a well-meaning sermon on the "holiness of dying" would be an outrage against those who must bear such terrors.

There are also ways of "daily death" that are results of abuse, cruelty or ignorance of others. These often do not transform human lives but crush them. We do not understand why God allows them to happen; the mystery of suffering is, perhaps, even greater – and demands from us an even greater trust – than the mystery of death. We must cling to our trust that all human death is blessed by God and that one day we may be allowed to see how it all "worked." We might be able to see that in the end "all will be well, and all will be well, and all manner of things will be well."[18]

We know, of course, that there have been many people who, firm in their faith, faced such deaths with acceptance and even joy. In all periods of history, martyrs died horribly, still praising the goodness of God. Others lived holy, Christ-like lives in the midst of hell. But these were great saints, men and women who had been called to such an end by God, and given the grace to accept it and even welcome it. Most of us are not asked for such a sacrifice, and we should never "nominate" ourselves for martyrdom, or choose a way of life to which we have not been called. This is why we pray – or should pray – every day for "peace in our day" and the grace of a "good" death: for a "merciful, peaceful and unafraid end of our earthly lives."[19]

Dying of Love

Although only a few are called to the death of martyrdom, all are called to the death of love. We are all called to die to self-love. The dying of love we mean here is not the dying "of a broken heart," in the sense in which we usually use that phrase. Some people may fall into depression and give up their desire to live – some may even die – due to some tragic loss or rejection. These are perhaps the greatest of human sorrows, but they are not caused by love. They are rather results of unfulfilled need. True love, the love of which we have all been called to die, is not based on need but on a surrender of need: on willingness to place the good of another above our own.

Most of us, I think, are very aware of how little we are capable of such love. We are too weak and too scared, we have too many desperate, often legitimate, needs to fulfill. We may be so busy serving ourselves, protecting ourselves from discomfort and harm, that we forget there are other human beings in even greater need. Perhaps we do keep trying to be less selfish, more aware of others, but so often we fail. When we realize this, we may become despondent, for we do not like thinking of ourselves as "failures" at love.

It is very important, however, to know the truth and allow ourselves to be stripped of the illusions we all build up about ourselves. When we begin to see ourselves as we truly are, we become more humble, more real, and more open to love. St. Paul said that "all things work for the good of those who love God." (Romans 8:28) This may sometimes seem to us to be an exercise in wishful thinking, an attempt to console ourselves for our failures at love or for the evil we have done. But it is not wishful thinking, it is the reality of every life of faith. God can indeed turn everything into good, into love: even our sins.

The important thing to do, however, is not to spend much time worrying about our imperfections and our failures at love, but to begin to love in the way that right now is possible for us. We must practise loving every day. We must "stretch" ourselves a little each day, do a little thing for somebody, forgive somebody, pray for somebody instead of nursing a grudge. We must try to give sometimes more than we can comfortably give, "go the extra mile" or even only an extra inch! Most of us can only die of love day by day, and inch by inch.

The Way of Forgiveness and Compassion

Above all, I think, we die of love by *forgiveness* and *compassion*. It is amazing how hard it is for us to forgive those who have offended or harmed us. Even when the offense has been a relatively minor one, we may be filled with a sense of violence done to us, and with feelings of outrage or resentment against those who have hurt or upset us. These feelings are very difficult for us to let go of, for every letting go, every act of forgiveness is, in a way, an act of *abdication* on our part: an admission that we are not of greatest importance in the world, and that evil done to us is not always a capital crime or an unforgivable offense. Each act of forgiveness, therefore, is "a little death"; each makes us a little less self-centred and a little more compassionate, more open to the needs and suffering of others.

The world is filled with suffering, and we can never really avoid seeing it or hearing about it. We may often want to shut our eyes, shut off the voices and close our hearts, for we feel we cannot bear any more pain. The immensity of human misery may threaten to overwhelm us; we may even fear that it can make us despair of the goodness of God. We just want to turn away and forget it all.

And yet, that is exactly what we must not do. We must never turn away from the suffering of others. We must help all we can, however little that may be. We must give "until it hurts," as Mother Teresa used to say, and because we know this is never enough, we must bear our helplessness, even if it breaks our hearts. Most of all, we must be *present* to other people's pain wherever they happen to be and we must bring it to God. We must remain at the foot of the world's cross crying out to God and *never* give up crying. Compassion is, I think, often the hardest, the most painful way of loving, for it offers no reward, no sense of "achievement" or self-importance; it fulfills no need of our own. It may embitter us if we attempt to walk it alone. True compassion is a grace and it can only be found in union with the infinite compassion and mercy of God.

The Greatest Gift

Although it is true, as Christ told us again and again, that we cannot love God unless we love our neighbour, it is also true that we cannot love our neighbour unless we love God.[20] "God is love," St. John tells us, and that means that God is the source of all love, and that without our participation in his life we cannot even begin to love. We cannot break out of our self-isolation and extend ourselves in loving anybody or anything, we cannot be *present* to anybody, unless we have already begun our life in God. We may not realize it, we may even deny it and insist that we do not believe in God, but the reality is that whenever we truly love, it means that we have already begun to love God.

But what do we mean when we say that we love God? What can we ever do for him? What can we offer him? The reality of our poverty in a relationship with God – who is infinitely rich, who does not need anything from us, who does not depend on us for anything – is such that we realize we cannot offer him anything at all except ourselves, our *presence*. This should make us humble, but it should also make us aware of the real value and beauty of the human person. For only a person can be truly aware of and present to another. Only a person can love. Presence is the greatest, perhaps the only necessary gift of love.

To be present to another is to be aware of his or her unique existence and to accept it unconditionally in an encounter of love. We long for such presence and acceptance and often feel that, without it, we shall die of loneliness. Yet, it is amazing how rarely we are truly present to one another, how little we are aware of one another. We look at others and say we love them, but we don't really *see* them; we only see what we need from them, what pleases us in them.

God, however, is always – *now* – aware of us and present to us. God's presence is *real* whether we know it or not, whether we believe in it or not. We do not need to "make it happen," for it is always there. All we need to do is to open ourselves to it and *learn* to be present to him. We need to be willing to trust him with ourselves, however "unworthy" or unready we may feel. Then perhaps we, too, shall be able to say what an old man once said to St. John Vianney, when he had asked the man what he did during all the hours he spent in church: "He looks at me, I look at him, and we are happy together."

If we learn to let God be present to us and "look" at us like that, if we learn to look at him like that, we shall have learned the secret of true prayer. For prayer, true prayer – whatever we ask God for, whatever words we use, or if we use no words at all – begins and ends in the presence of God. Prayer is our small, finite presence, open and attentive to the infinite presence of God. Such prayer is love; it is heaven already on earth.

Prayer of the Presence

When we think of prayer, we sometimes think of it in such beggarly terms. We think of "saying our prayers," carrying out certain "pious" devotions or fulfilling our "holy obligation." We think of asking God to give us what we need, to protect us from danger or deliver us from evil. Sometimes when we pray we remember to praise him and thank him for what he has done for us but, most often, we simply badger him for this or that. There is nothing wrong with badgering God – Christ told us that we should. But what is not so good is to forget, as we often do, that the only thing we truly need is to be in God's *presence* and to be *present* to him.

We are usually so absorbed in ourselves, in what we do, in what we think, in what is happening to us, or in what might happen to us, that we leave ourselves little time or opportunity for remembering God. God, however, always remembers us and will not let us forget him for too long. Sometimes, for a split second, we might see him in the beauty of things: in nature, in a beloved face, in a work of art. We might hear him in great music, in our children's voices, in a bird's song or the sound of rain. We might come upon his presence unawares in the midst of a most ordinary activity and suddenly we know what it is that has touched us, and why it is that we must always search for God.

Whenever we remember that we are in God's presence, whenever we have a glimpse of him, we realize, without any hesitation or doubt, that there is no other "place" – in time or in eternity – where we shall ever want to be. In God's presence, our minds are silent and clear, our hearts are at peace, our bodies are relaxed, and we are filled with joy. We are at home in our bodies, at home in the world, and we know we shall be at home in heaven as well. We know that our sins and failures, however great they may be, will dissolve in his presence like smoke! The presence of God is our life, our eternity, our true and final home.

True prayer, "prayer of the presence," is the "royal" way of dying of love. It puts us, as it were, in the spiritual space in which we shall find ourselves at the moment of death, when we have left behind everything we know, everything we have – even life itself – and stand before God, empty-handed, aware of our total poverty, relying on nothing but love. Whenever we are in the presence of God, we place ourselves on the very threshold of the mystery of death, we surrender ourselves to him, we "lose our life" and enter eternal life.

And that is true of *everything* we do in life! Every action, every breath, every feeling or thought: if we bring it into the presence of God, if we surrender it to him, it becomes for us "a little entrance" to eternity, the door of the Kingdom. At work or at rest, awake or asleep, happy or miserable, we enter divine presence at the heart of all things. We become aware of each moment and we learn to let it go; we throw ourselves into the hands of the Living God and *we learn to die.*

Practice for Death

Most of us are probably aware that early Christians, as well as monks down the ages – non-Christian and Christian alike – considered it necessary to be always conscious of the reality and inevitability of death, to meditate on it often, and even to expose themselves to situations that would make death more present to them. Some of these practices – for example, praying for long hours at cemeteries, observing and reflecting on the process of dissolution, keeping human skulls in their cells – may appear to us strange, morbid, perhaps distasteful, and even psychologically and emotionally dangerous. We cannot even imagine ourselves "practising" death in that way.

And yet, these ancient traditions have something of value to teach us. They remind us that it is important that we should not allow ourselves to forget the reality of death, that we should resist our society's pressure to deny death. We, too, must prepare for death in order that we can meet it with courage and in peace. We, too, must find a way of practising death.

A friend told me of a recent experience she had. After reading a story of a saint who had tried to live every day as if it was the last day of his life, she decided it would be interesting to try doing this herself. And so, that evening, as she got into bed, she began to plan her last day on earth. She thought about what she would do, whom she would see, whom she would ask to forgive her, to whom she would say goodbye. She began to feel quite sorry for herself, and even reduced herself to tears, but in the end she realized she was just playing a game, so she gave it up and went to sleep.

The next morning, however, as she woke up, a very clear thought came into her mind. "What would I do," she asked herself, "if I knew that I was dying *now*, this minute, that I had only a few more *seconds* to live?" Suddenly, it was no longer a game. She was really there, at the End, alone, and there was no time left to prepare or plan. There was nothing she could do or undo. And the most astonishing thing was, she said, that after a split second of panic she knew exactly what she must do. *Lord, have mercy on me, a sinner!* she heard herself cry.

This experience was, my friend believed, one of the greatest graces she had ever received. She realized, that, for her, there was only one way of dying, and one way of "practising" it: to throw herself into the arms of God, not only at the end of life, but *every day*, and cry for mercy. To do it so insistently, so constantly, that the prayer that came to her spontaneously at the moment of her "death experience," as she called it, would become a ceaseless prayer of her heart, that it would shape her life as well as her death. What my friend discovered, in fact, was the fundamental insight of Christianity: the belief in our total dependence – in death as in life – on the infinite mercy of God.

Mercy

Belief in God's mercy is not an option for Christians; it is the most important reality of our faith. Although there may be many ways of expressing and living this reality, the truth of it must remain the cornerstone of our lives and the source of all our trust. For, as Christ told us again and again, there are no limits to God's mercy: to his willingness to search for us when we are lost, to forgive and heal us when we have sinned. There is no end to his willingness to love us.

We tend to think of the mercy of God as his "pity" for us, for which we have to beg, for which we have to humiliate ourselves and wait trembling and afraid. This is an awful distortion of the Good News. It is a lie, and to believe it is to deny the truth that Christ died a horrible death to reveal: the truth of God's infinite and unconditional mercy. To ask for mercy is not to cringe in self-abasement or fear, but to look towards God in trust and hope. Mercy is a "summary" of all we know or need to know about God's love for us. It manifests God's presence to us and his awareness of us at every moment of our lives and his acceptance of us as we truly are: created in his image, destined to share his glory, but weak and prone to failure and fear. When we ask for mercy we ask to be made whole again: to be filled with God. We ask for healing and love.[21]

Human words are incapable of expressing the reality of God's love; we can only speak of it in analogies, images or metaphors. We can only speak of "aspects" of this love: presence, awareness, mercy. But God has no aspects, he just *is*; he is indivisible and always one. Even to say that God "loves us" – if we think of loving as something God "does" – may dim for us the light of this great mystery. God *is* presence, he *is* mercy, he *is* love.

Thus, when we speak of God's "mercy and love" we mean one immense overflowing of his divine being – of who he is. We can perhaps say that God's mercy is his love made "safe" for us: the only way we can experience this love while we are still on earth without being crushed by the immensity and power of it. If God revealed his love to us in all its burning fullness, if he came to us in all his divine glory, we could not open ourselves to it: it would blind us and overwhelm our minds. And so, God chose to show us his love "dimly," gently, in the mercy he offers us every moment of our lives and which he will surely not refuse us at the hour of death.

Justice

It is sometimes said that, as Christians, we are asked to embrace two contradictory beliefs. On the one hand, we must hold to our unconditional trust in God's infinite mercy and reject any shadow of a doubt that it might ever be refused to us. On the other, we are taught, by Christ himself, that we must face judgment, both right after death and at the end of time: that there is a "heaven" and a "hell." We are told, again and again, that we should always be watchful, for we "do not know the day or the hour" when we shall die. We must pray ceaselessly that we may not have to face that hour unrepentant and unforgiven. We are even told to *fear* God. How can we reconcile these two "truths"?

Our minds do not like paradoxes. When faced with one we, like computers fed two contradictory bits of information, cannot process it. We tend to conclude, therefore, that only one side of the paradox can be true, or, if both must be true, they cannot be true at the same time. Some, of course, will solve the problem by simply denying the existence of hell, and the need to fear God at all. Others will insist that God is always just, and, therefore, he cannot show mercy to those who do not "deserve" it. Others will say that God's justice always causes him to be angry with the sinner but, because he is merciful, he can be persuaded to change his mind. Still others claim that heaven and hell are manifestations of the two "sides" or aspects of God: his mercy is found in heaven, but his justice rules hell!

Yet, as we have seen, there can be no "sides" or aspects of God. God is one and he is love. Both his mercy and his justice *are* his love. Both heaven and hell, therefore, must also be manifestations of love. We cannot, of course, understand this mystery, for it is bigger than our thought. It is veiled from our eyes for it could destroy us if we saw it unveiled. Thus, we must "fear" it; we must stand in awe of it. To fear God means to be filled with awe at the mystery of his love.

But, although we cannot understand the mystery, we can perhaps glimpse a shadow of its meaning if we contemplate it, as the Fathers of the Church always did, in the "mirror" of what they considered the greatest gift of the human person: the gift of freedom. As St. Irenaeus said in the second century, "Man is rational and therefore like God; he is created with free will and is master over his acts."[22]

Because we are "rational" beings – created in the image of God – because we can think and understand the consequences of our acts, God's justice should not be viewed as a sentence imposed on us from outside, as it were, but as consequences of the choices we, ourselves, have made. "The origin of evil lies in the liberty of the being who accomplishes it," wrote the great Orthodox theologian V. Lossky.[23] And therein also lies the origin of good. Thus, to the extent to which we are rational and in full possession of our faculties, we can and must exercise our liberty. We choose heaven or hell.

The Gift of Freedom

This truth may be difficult for us to understand at first. We may feel that such radical choices are beyond our capacity to make: that we are too ignorant, too confused or too weak to make them. Nevertheless, it is the central teaching of Christianity, as well as a fundamental principle of all moral life, that *we are free to choose our final destiny*. However difficult our lives have been, however wounded we have become by events and tragedies that befell us, this essential freedom has never been taken from us: in the final analysis, we are responsible for ourselves. We are responsible for our every act, every thought and word, for they all flow from the fundamental choice we are called to make every day: God or not-God, love or not-love.

This truth is so important that to deny it, even implicitly – by the way we conduct our lives, by the way we allow ourselves to be manipulated by our own laziness and fear, or by the way we justify ourselves and blame others – is the greatest spiritual danger in our life of faith. It is easy for us to slide into it. Most people around us seem to be convinced, and eager to convince us, that the freedom we believe we have is an illusion, an attempt to make ourselves feel better, to give meaning to our lives. They seem eager to convince us that everything we think, say or do is determined by the external and internal pressures under which we live: that we are only what we are "programmed" to be.

What makes this claim especially difficult to resist is the fact that such thoughts and doubts often invade our own minds. It is much easier to believe in determinism, which claims to deal only with "facts," than to believe in freedom, which is a spiritual reality and thus cannot be "proven" to exist.

We may also be tempted to embrace determinism by the fear of freedom and responsibility with which many of us struggle all our lives. We may find it difficult to make decisions and are terrified of making a wrong choice. We may resent the degree of spiritual effort that freedom and responsibility demand from us. Our spiritual sloth – one of the "deadly" sins – makes us especially vulnerable to the temptation of drifting through life as if we had no choice.

And yet, if we do not resist this temptation with all the strength we have, we shall lose everything that makes our lives worthwhile. If there is no free will, there can be no holiness and no sin. Without freedom, morality is an illusion and good and evil only two sides of an absurd universe; joy is a by-product of pleasure, and human suffering bad luck or a dreadful mistake. In such a universe God is not love, but either a tyrant, an idea, or a blind "force." If there is no freedom, there is no love.

Freedom of Repentance

This is why the Christian Church ceaselessly calls us to repentance: to a conversion of heart and will. The call to repentance, in the true Christian sense of the word, is not a call to self-hatred or guilt, but a call to freedom, to a struggle against the chains of habit, weakness and fear which bind us so often. When we repent, we refuse to be cowed by all the voices that shout at us from outside or within ourselves, voices that tell us that we are not responsible for who we are and what we do, that we are slaves of circumstances, helpless victims of what has been done to us.

Repentance is our way of embracing our freedom, of "practising" it, of celebrating it, of rejoicing in the victory of God's mercy over human sloth and sin. Every moment we become aware of how unfree we have been, every time we cry, "Lord have mercy on me!" we shake off our passivity and fear. When we repent, as we have already seen, we "deny self": we break out of our self-constriction and open ourselves to love. Repentance is our expression of trust, not in ourselves but in him who has made us free, and of realization that when we come before the face of God, when we enter the divine presence, when we lose ourselves in him, we are always – at every moment and in eternity – free to choose.

It is for this reason that repentance, as my friend discovered, can also be our best practice for death, for the final choosing we shall be asked to make at the doors of eternity. For it is possible to believe, I think, that, at the End, when we face Christ in all his divine power and beauty, when we see the immense, unimaginable promise of our own humanity, this irreversible gift of our freedom will be presented to us in its glorious fullness. Of course, all the choices we have made throughout our life on earth – or which we have refused to make – may weigh heavily on us. The voice of the Accuser within us may try to tell us that it is now too late to change.

But if we resist that final temptation, refuse to listen to that lying voice, we shall surely see that it is not too late, that the doors of God's infinite mercy can never be closed to us. We shall realize that even now we can turn away from all our tragedies and disasters, our errors and doubts, all our sins: that we can repent for them and leave them all to the mercy of God – and that we are still free to choose. If we want God, we choose him – that is heaven. If we do not want him, we choose ourselves – that is hell. It is, I believe, as simple as that.

Judgment

Yet, simple or not, there is no doubt that the thought of meeting God at the moment of death must still fill us with apprehension and fear, perhaps even with terror. How can a finite being see Infinity and live? How can we look on the face of God and not be crushed by the Truth and Beauty suddenly thrust upon us? How can we feel comfortable and safe when we pass beyond space and time, beyond any imaginable reality? When we can no longer hide behind any concepts, clever words or self-serving deceptions? When we are stripped of all excuses and all disguises and come, at last, to *see* – fully, totally – our own weakness, our helplessness and our abysmal poverty? When we become, indeed, the "poorest of the poor"?

This process of stripping may yet prove most difficult for those of us who have considered ourselves "religious," even devout. At the moment of death, we may suddenly have to realize how often we had been only "covering" ourselves with religion, putting it on as a cloak to hide our nakedness, our disbelief, our lack of love or our fear. The ardour of our devotions, the loudness of our proclamations, the ease with which we condemned "the world," and the tendency to count ourselves among the "elect" may have been, at least to some degree, a way of seeking approval and acceptance of others, or an escape from a sense of inadequacy and fear.

We may have to understand that our religion has not always been an expression of our love for God, but rather of fear. It may have been an "insurance policy" against the judgment we have always known we must face one day, and which is now upon us. Perhaps we have not yet learned to rely only on the mercy of him who is Perfect Love and have believed that we must deserve heaven by our own efforts and virtues, and now we see that this we can never do. Perhaps we have not yet understood that the only good way to die is the way of the "Good Thief" who, after a life of rebellion and sin knew enough to cry at the end: "Jesus, remember me when you come into your kingdom!"

We have all failed to reach the perfection to which we have been called. In the meeting with our Lord and our Judge which awaits us, we are all unworthy to untie the strap of his shoes. The moment of death will take us to the very core of our reality, to the centre of our being, and we shall finally realize, beyond any doubt, who we truly are, what we truly believe, what we truly love. This realization is our Judgment. It is our reward or our punishment, our heaven or our hell.

Hell

When I was a young woman, I could not believe in hell, because I could not believe that anybody could be afraid of love, could reject love. Everybody I knew, including myself, seemed to be always looking for it and bemoaning its absence. I was, therefore, convinced that regardless of how wicked and unloving we have been in life, at the moment of death, when we are given a glimpse of the immense love of God, we would *all* embrace it, surrender ourselves to it and thus find ourselves in heaven. Nobody would ever choose to go to hell!

Now I know better. I have learned how difficult it is for most of us to accept love – real love: love that is unconditional, that does not expect anything in return except love. Such love often makes us uncomfortable, afraid, because it calls us to respond in a way that seems to threaten our "selfhood," to step out from behind our self-imposed boundaries and defenses; to demand from us more than we can or want to give. To respond to love – even human love – we must decrease a little, we must die a little. Love is very dangerous to the self. How much more dangerous must Infinite Love be!

We may find this difficult to believe, especially if

all our lives we have considered ourselves "social" beings, fond of the company of others. We may have found it easy to love and be loved. We may have been charitable and generous, always ready to support good causes with our money and time. And yet, in the end, we too may have to realize how small and constricted our many loves have been, how little we were really willing to share of ourselves. Our "easy loving" may have been our way of protecting ourselves against the danger of real love: a love that might have broken our hearts and thus made them ready for God.

On the other hand, we may have been "loners," perhaps through shyness, or through a fear of rejection and pain, and may have convinced ourselves that we preferred to be alone. We may have even considered it to be a virtue, a vocation to "renounce" human love in order to love "only God." But at the moment of death, when it seems that the goal is almost within reach, when an eternity of "nothing but God" seems just around the corner, we may suddenly have to realize that there is no hope – on earth or in heaven – of ever loving only God! Heaven is filled with people for us to love!

And so, it no longer seems to me impossible to believe that at the end, when we meet him who *is* love, when infinite love is poured out on us without measure, without conditions, as pure gift, when we are invited to enter irreversibly into an eternity of love, we may panic, we may refuse, we may withdraw behind the walls of self and wish to be left alone, on our own: in hell. When we close ourselves to love, we are trapped in the prison of our own self and burn in the fire of resentment and fear. When we reject love, we reject heaven and choose hell.

Eternity of Hell

Yet, if "going to hell" is not a punishment imposed on us by an angry God but a choice of each individual human being, is it conceivable that *any* human choice could be "eternal"? Is it possible for human beings *never* to change their mind? And if they do, how could God refuse to grant mercy to those who beg for it, even those in hell? How could he refuse to listen to their pleas at any time or at least at the Last Judgment at the end of time? How could we reconcile such a belief with the belief in the infinite mercy of God?

These are very difficult and painful questions. It is important, I think, to realize that they have been asked again and again, since the beginning of Christianity. Some theologians concluded that, because God was love, he could not refuse mercy to anybody, at any time. All those who begged for forgiveness – even those in hell – would have it granted to them. A few went so far as to believe that not even one person would be left in hell at the end. We hope and pray that this may indeed prove true. Yet, however difficult it may be for us to conceive of any person continuing to reject God for eternity, we should not forget that it is *possible* for a human being to do so. The "final chance" may be offered, but the freedom to refuse it cannot ever be taken away.

We should also remind ourselves that, like all matters of faith, hell is a mystery that cannot be solved by any effort of the human mind, any appeal to logic or any theological argument. In this, as in all other painful questions with which the Christian tradition confronts us, we cannot *think* our way to truth. We cannot ever be freed from the need to believe. The only "answer" to the problem of hell lies in placing all our trust in God's infinite and compassionate love.

One thing, however, is beyond any doubt: we are not allowed to conclude that anybody has gone or will go to hell. In fact, we are forbidden to think that of any person or group, however wicked and depraved they may seem to us. We must never presume to think that we can know how any person has "survived," or will survive, his final meeting with God. All we are told, and all we need to know, is that it is possible for a person to refuse to choose love. We may pray and, I think, we may hope that in the end no one will ever choose such a dreadful singularity. I know that *I* must pray that *I* may not choose it. It is a terrifying possibility, and it is essential never to forget that it exists.

The Bright Spring of Joy

When we refuse to surrender ourselves to love, it is most often because we are afraid of the pain it might bring us. And, of course, it is often painful to break down the protective barriers we have set up around ourselves, to walk out of a prison we have lived in all our lives, to enter into a relationship with another. Especially if this "another" is God, who may ask of us what we least want to give, who may ask us to bear much suffering, even death, for love.

But we are not always asked to walk the way of pain. Sometimes the death of self comes to us in a surrender to happiness, in creative activity, in the discipline of work we do well, in beauty and in joy. Joy forces us out of our little self so that we can grow into a bigger one. Joy makes it impossible for us to stay cowering in our corner, to go on feeling alienated, rejected, alone. Joy connects us with the whole of creation and allows the grace of God to flow over us, to heal us and transform us. Joy is a sign of God's presence, of his coming to free us from bondage, to call us out of the prison of our small self, to *divinize* us. Joy is our fullest answer to the beauty and love of God. When we refuse love, we refuse not only suffering but, above all, joy.

Joy and suffering are not mutually exclusive. The great Christian mystery of suffering is that when suffering and even death are accepted creatively – *when* we do not simply passively *bear* them, but *embrace* them as God's will and signs of his action in us – they do not destroy joy, but deepen it. Suffering and death can always be open to joy; they can become for us a "bright spring" of joy.

Contemporary Western Christians are not, on the whole, sufficiently aware of this truth. Perhaps because we tend to treat joy and pleasure as synonymous, deep down in our minds we still consider all pleasure suspect. Perhaps because we tend to see nothing but evil in suffering, and view death as the greatest evil of all, we do not really want to believe that they could be life-giving and a source of joy, and so our fear of pain keeps us in chains. We do not consider heaven – if we believe in it at all – as worth suffering and dying for!

Heaven

Many of us have a misguided and puny idea of heaven. We may think of heaven as of a place to which we hope we shall go, which we shall enter as a reward for all the good deeds we have done on earth. Heaven, we seem to think, simply transfers us from this earthly reality, this "valley of tears," into a reality that is wonderful and beautiful, where everybody is happy, where there is no more suffering and pain. Even when we believe that heaven is "where we see God" we often think of it as seeing him, as it were, outside of ourselves, of standing *before* him and looking *at* him out of our own ordinary eyes.

Heaven, however, is not a "place" to which we go, but a reality we must *become*. Heaven is eternal life – life of God which has become our life too. In other words, we "enter" heaven by the process we have already described: by denying self and becoming "another Christ," that is by becoming divinized, one with God. In heaven, God is "all in all," (1 Corinthians 15:28) which means that *love* is all in all, and, unless we too have become love, there is no room for us in heaven. We simply cannot fit in there.

Yet, in the Christian Tradition, becoming one

with God is never understood as "merging" with him and ceasing to exist as fully aware, individual persons. God is always, timelessly, aware of us and present to us, but we, too, in our small, finite way, remain present to him and aware of him. Union with God is a *communion of persons.* Without presence, without personal awareness, there could be no heaven as Christians understand it; there could only be "Emptiness" – boundless peace, perhaps, but it would not be *eternal life* of each.

We are often, I think, attracted to ways of belief that seem to offer us a possibility of leaving behind what we perceive to be the bonds of our personal awareness, of our own individual self. We long, perhaps, to merge with the Divine Self, the divine oneness, to "plunge" into God and disappear. Our limited, small "selves" may seem to be a terrible burden to us, our personality a form of conditioned reflex, our finiteness a slavery. We cringe at the idea that we might carry this burden with us into eternity.

But being a person means much more than having a personality or an individual "self." God revealed himself to us as Person (or, more exactly, as a Communion of Persons: the Holy Trinity) and thus we understand that our personal existence – our "personhood" – is an indelible image – an icon – of the Personhood of God. It is as persons that we enter heaven and experience the presence of God.

We embrace infinity not by merging with it, dissolving in it, but only by the union of our finiteness with God, through love.

If we understand love in the way Christians understand it, we cannot view our personhood as a prison from which we must long to be liberated. As an Orthodox monk pointed out to me a few years ago, being a person can only seem constraining if we view it from any other perspective than love. It is through the self-emptying love of Christ – which we also make our own – that each created person is offered the possibility of "extending" and embracing Infinity.

Of course, our human understanding of what it means to be a divinized person, what it means to be a "presence" risen with Christ and seated with him in glory, what it means to be a *saint*, is always totally inadequate. We do not know what personhood will mean in a reality beyond earthly space and time, when there are no more words, no more concepts, no more illusion and sin. We cannot ever comprehend what it will be like to see God, not in the mirror of our minds and imaginations, not in the darkness of faith but "face to face"; what it will mean to be totally penetrated by the presence of God, to be totally in love. The mystery of heaven is the mystery of the Communion of Saints: of God present at the heart of reality, and of each human person present to God and to each other in Christ.

Communion of Saints

Because we cannot love God without loving one another, Communion of Saints also means being in communion with every human being who has ever lived. Saints are those who have opened themselves completely to the infinite love of God and allowed it to pour through them onto every person they meet, everything they touch. Saints are in communion not only with angels and other saints, but with everybody and everything. They are open to the whole of creation.

Communion of saints is not a "doctrine" we "must" believe because it is a part of our Creed, but a reality of love we must live. It is not a teaching about saints who have "departed" and gone to heaven, but an awareness of their living presence. It is a "living intercourse between persons": present, past and future, made possible to us by the presence – beyond space and time – of the Holy Spirit in each.[24] Communion of Saints is eternal life of heaven already present to us and in us; it is the true life of the Church.

The Church on earth, however human and sinful it may appear to us to be, participates already in the life of the Church in heaven. The Church is a communion of persons, the living and the dead. We are all connected, present to each other, supporting each other, sharing all the gifts and treasures of our faith. And, above all, we have the Holy Spirit: the gift of the presence of God. This is the essential reality of our faith. Christ is among us and we are one with the heavenly Church.

And what about our own dead? It is surprising how rarely most of us, although we claim to believe in "eternal life," think of our dead as actually present to us. We remember them and mourn them, we think of them with love – or, sometimes, with pain and regret – but we do not really believe in their presence with us. We think it is too late to get to know them better, to love them more, or to be reconciled with them. Why is it too late? What is to prevent us from getting to know those who have already died? Why is it too late to form a relationship with them? Why is it too late to forgive, and be forgiven? Our dead have not gone from us: they, too, are within the Communion of Saints; they pray for us, we pray for them and our relationship continues. Love does not end with death.

Love Beyond Death

One powerful expression of this love – prayers for the dead – has been a part of Christian Teaching from earliest times. Because the dead remain alive in the sight of God, because in eternity death has no meaning, our prayers and good actions offered for them can help them, although in ways known only to God. This truth still remains an integral part of both Catholic and Orthodox teaching, although the two Churches differ somewhat in the way they approach it.

The Catholic Church has, since the thirteenth century at least, taught the existence of Purgatory – a "place" or rather a "state" in which many souls of the faithful, if not most, find themselves after death.[25] These souls have never denied or rejected their faith or, by evil actions, cut themselves off from the Communion of Saints. They have not rejected love, they have not chosen hell. But, during their lifetime, they may not have opened themselves fully to the work of grace, they may not have loved enough, and are not yet ready to enter fully into the presence of God. They still need to be purified. This they "do" in purgatory, before the Last Judgment when, presumably, all "purgation" will be completed and all will be admitted to the company of saints.

The Orthodox, on the other hand, have always been unwilling to commit themselves to any "definitions" and explanations of spiritual realities that are not clearly sanctioned by Scripture or by the teachings of the Fathers and other great saints. They do not believe that purgatory has such "credentials," and thus, the majority of Orthodox theologians appear to reject its existence. The Orthodox Church, although it always insists on the need and importance of praying for the dead, prefers to remain silent on how God deals with the sins and imperfections of those who die in the faith. If one persists in the discussion of this issue, they may quote the words of the Great St. Anthony, who when he was once worrying about a similar question, suddenly heard a voice saying to him, "Anthony, attend to yourself; for these are the judgments of God, and it is not for you to know them."[26]

Yet, whether we are Catholic or Orthodox, we all have the same work of love to do: to pray for those who have gone before us, as they pray for us. We must remain present to them, as they are to us. Death does not divide us, does not make us inaccessible to each other; we share the same reality of love.

The Hour

We already share in the eternal reality of love, but we are also still here, on this earth, in this moment of time. We still have our dying to do. And, however hard we "practise" our death, however deeply we reflect on it and pray about it, we shall still have to face it not knowing what it will be like and probably very afraid. Yet our faith assures us that we shall not have to face it alone and without help.

The Church accompanies us and supports us every step of the way. Our friends and relatives gather around us to keep us company, to pray with us and for us, when we can no longer pray for ourselves. Candles are lit as a sign of Christ's presence and victory over every death. We are anointed with holy oils as a pledge of salvation and receive communion – the *viaticum* – our "journey bread." We are "passed on" by the Church on earth into the hands of the Church in heaven; we are plunged into the Communion of Saints.

Angels are summoned to lead and help us, and so are all the saints. The Mother of God stands by us, as she stood by the Cross. We who have prayed to her all our lives will not forget to ask for her protection "at the hour of our death." She who is the Mother of all surely cannot forsake us at the moment of our greatest need. Because we are sinners, because we have failed again and again, she will console us and remind us of the infinite mercy that awaits us now. She who is called the *Gate of Heaven* will see us safely through.

And when at last we *are* through, when our journey is finished and our dying is done, the Church will bury us with prayers and lights, with singing and the ringing of bells. The priest will sanctify our body with incense and bless it with the holy cross. Our friends will come to "pay their respects" and to say goodbye. They shall carry us to the cemetery and cover us with earth. They will place flowers at our graves and perhaps they will cry. And that is how it should be. We have been around for a while, we have loved them, they have loved us, and now we must go.

This is the way Christians have died for centuries. We should try to make sure that it will still be the way we are allowed to go. We must not permit our strange, frightened world to make our dying as insignificant and unobtrusive as it wants to make it. Our death is not insignificant. It is the greatest hour of our earthly lives, it is our entrance into eternity and our meeting with God. And our grave, the tomb in which we are finally laid to rest, is holy ground, for it is a sign not of defeat but of victory. It is an icon of Christ's own glorious tomb.

The Empty Tomb

As we pray and reflect on our own death, and as we approach the end of our earthly life, we begin to realize more and more clearly what immense significance the tomb of Christ, the Empty Tomb, has for us. Because we have been "baptized into Christ's death," because we have "died with him and are buried with him," his tomb is also our final resting place. It is there that our death is conquered, our sins are laid to rest and we are made holy and ready for heaven. It is from there that we shall "rise with him" in glory. The tomb of Christ, perhaps we can say, is the place of our purification, the waiting-room of heaven.

Western Christians, on the whole, pay little attention to the Empty Tomb. If we think of it at all, it is as of a place where Christ was laid for a short while, a site in the Holy Land: a place to visit, once in a lifetime perhaps, but not really relevant to our own lives. We remember the events of Christ's death, burial, and resurrection, but the Mystery of the Empty Tomb – of God triumphant in the place of death – has practically disappeared from our consciousness, as it has disappeared from our liturgies, even during Holy Week. We think much about Christ's suffering and pain and finally his death, but we hardly ever think of his tomb. We leave Christ dead on Good Friday, as it were; we seal the door and go away. We do not remember him much, till we see him risen again on Easter Sunday.[27]

The Orthodox Tradition, on the other hand, has remained very clear and emphatic on this point. It is very significant, I think, that in the life of the Orthodox Church, although the Cross is always exalted and deeply venerated, it is the Empty Tomb that stands as the great symbol of the Passion. This is clearly seen in all her Liturgies, but especially in the Liturgies of the Holy Week.

How meaningful is this reverence for the tomb of Christ and how unfailingly it leads us into the heart of the mystery of death! The Liturgy of the Burial of Christ on the evening of Good Friday, his image stretched in the stillness of death, the mourning, the waiting – how *right* it seems! The descent of Christ to the dead, the breaking down of the gates of hell, the light penetrating the darkness of death, the confusion and the despair of the Enemy: how the Orthodox Church lives it, how she sings it, how she glories in it! How incredibly powerful, how *joyful*, is the Resurrection when it breaks out of darkness, out of hell, out of the night of death!

And how profoundly meaningful is the Empty Tomb as the sign of our own transformation and our resurrection. For, at the end, when we lie prostrate at the gap of death, afraid and totally "undone," we shall surely see that all the little daily deaths we have undergone, all the little tombs we have entered, have been but steps into this one glorious Tomb. We shall rest there, on the rock of his death, until "all is accomplished," all hope is fulfilled, the world is reborn, and we are summoned to meet God face to face.

Resurrection

The Christian hope of the "world reborn" is founded on the belief in the Second Coming of Christ to judge and restore all things, so that God can be "all in all." The final act of the drama of salvation will not be an act of destruction – as often it is expected to be – but of *resurrection*. The end of the world as we know it and its rebirth in glory will begin with the resurrection of every human being who has ever lived. The belief in the final *bodily* resurrection "on the last day" is fundamental to Christianity and has been clearly taught from the very beginning. To deny it is to throw every other aspect of the Christian teaching into serious doubt. If our hope of resurrection is in vain, St. Paul insisted, then our whole faith is in vain.

Belief in the resurrection of the body seems to be so difficult for many contemporary Christians to accept: so shocking, so embarrassing even, that they tend to ignore it, to reinterpret it in more "acceptable" symbolic terms, or even to deny it. They may prefer to view it as a "parable": an effort of the mind to imagine the unimaginable and to express eternal life of the spirit in a "bodily" form. They might argue that it is immortality of the soul or spirit that is the significant object of faith, that the body is only an "outer" aspect of life, a visible material "casing" for an invisible spirit: necessary for life in this world, but surely redundant in eternity.

Such a "reinterpretation" of Christian belief is not always only an attempt to make it more "rational," more acceptable to the modern scientific mind. It may also be due to a tendency, a *temptation*, constant throughout the history of the Church, to treat the body as an *inferior part* of the human person, even as sinful and bad – as a *prison* of the spirit. If we think of our bodies in such a negative and fundamentally non-Christian way, then the very idea that this inferior aspect of ourselves, this prison, should prove to be our fate for eternity – our sentence for time without end – may truly horrify us.

But as we have seen, Christian Tradition insists that in order to enter eternal life it is necessary for us to become "like Christ," which means to live and die with him but also to rise with him – in the body, as he did. It will be our body, "and not a hair of it will be lost," said St. Macarius. Yet it will also be changed, for "freed from the grossness of the fallen flesh, the resurrection body, will share in the qualities of Christ's human body at the Transfiguration and after the Resurrection."[28] After his resurrection, the disciples found it difficult to recognize Christ at first. He was somehow different, and yet he was also the same. He talked and ate with them, he walked with them, he touched them, he was seen ascending into heaven.

He now "sits at the Father's right hand," Man-God "world without end." He will come again, and then we too shall be "raised" in the fullness of our humanity and glorified with him forever.

Unimaginable End

We may find this insistence on the physical resurrection disturbing, we may find it impossible to believe, we may simply refuse to take it seriously. We shall never be able to understand it. Is it, however, any more "incredible" than the Incarnation? More difficult to believe than our own transformation into Christ or our individual "survival" of death? It is all one seamless reality: either possible or impossible to believe. But if we do believe it, what an immense view opens before our eyes! What a world of unimaginable hope!

We cannot yet understand or even imagine how such a resurrected being – a divinized, glorified person – will look, or function, or live. We do not know how the resurrected world will "work." We cannot imagine how "what is sown corruptible" will be raised "incorruptible." (1 Corinthians 15:42) But we do not need to know or imagine it. All we need to know and to believe is that the Scriptures shall be fulfilled; that there will be an "event" in time (or outside time, we cannot tell) when we shall be called back into the fullness of our body/soul/spirit life, and shall meet our Lord and our Judge face to face: that we shall face judgment, a fact which may now fill us with fear but which, our faith assures us, will not be a judgment of anger and condemnation but only of mercy and love. It will not crush us, but heal and restore us to life.

At the End, we believe, the old world will be consumed by the fire of God's presence finally unveiled, and there will be a "new heaven and a new earth." All things will be reborn in a morning of a new age, and we shall see with our human eyes, hear with our human ears, touch with our human hands and experience with our human hearts a reality beyond anything we can ever in this life know or understand: a glory and beauty beyond anything we can ever imagine, a love beyond any we have ever hoped or longed for. Then, at last, our journey will come to an end, the door to eternity will be thrown open forever, and there will be no more pain or fear or tears, but only infinite love and an overflowing joy.

Notes

1   This is important to realize, because religious people, particularily in our "scientific" age, have often been tempted to make spiritual reality more "believable" by attempting to reconcile it with scientific thinking of the time. Thus, at present, some argue that modern physics, with its post-Newtonian view of matter and energy, has made it possible to view spiritual reality as a form of "energy" or "force" and, therefore, as an aspect of the "natural" universe, although in a manner not yet understood. Spiritual reality, they hope, may one day be "legitimized" by science.

From a religious perspective, however, spiritual reality cannot be equated with any aspect of physical reality. In other words, belief in eternity – or in any other aspect of spiritual reality – will never be established by scientific enquiry, but will always remain an object of faith. We shall never be freed from the necessity to "stretch" ourselves beyond where scientific inquiry can take us.

2   *Catechism of the Catholic Church* (CCC) no. 363.

3   This wonderful phrase was used recently by a 93-year-old woman in a letter to *Parabola* magazine (Winter 1999, p. 138).

4   cf. Elisabeth Kübler-Ross, *On Death and Dying.*

5   Discussed in detail in Fr. Seraphim Rose, *The Soul After Death,* published by the Herman of Alaska Brotherhood, 1980. Note that many Orthodox disagree with his views on the afterlife presented there.

6   *Mother Maria: Her Life and Letters,* edited by Sister Thekla (London: Darton, Longman and Todd, 1979, pp. 118-119). Mother Maria (Lydia Gysi) was an Orthodox nun and foundress of the Monastery of the Assumption in North Yorkshire in England, where she died in 1977. Although I never met Mother Maria, her thought has greatly influenced me. I have written about her and my "meeting" with her in *Encounter with a Desert Mother,* published by Peregrina Publishing Co., Toronto, Ontario, 1997. Chapter 6 of that book provided the original inspiration for this present work.

7   Bishop Kallistos Ware, *The Orthodox Way*, St. Vladimir's Seminary Press, 1996, pp. 133-134.

8   S.Th. II–II (see CCC no. 155).

9   cf. *Catechism of the Catholic Church,* no. 170.

10   Catherine Doherty was born in Russia in 1896, from where she escaped after the Revolution. She came to Canada in 1929, where she worked with the poor during the Great Depression, first in Toronto and then in Harlem. In 1947 she and her husband, Edward Doherty, a well-known reporter, came to Combermere, a small rural community in Ontario, Canada. There she founded the Madonna House Apostolate, a community of lay women, men and priests dedicated to "living the Gospel without a compromise." She died in 1985. The Apostolate now has more than 200 members – in Combermere and in

over twenty field houses scattered throughout Canada, the United States and overseas. Catherine Doherty wrote many books, the best known being, perhaps, *Poustinia* (a Russian word for "desert"), published in 1975 by Ave Maria Press. The book describes the way of life of Russian *poustiniks* or hermits – a way of prayer and love – and suggests how ordinary men and women can incorporate it into their everyday lives in the contemporary world.

11 *De Spiritu Sancto*, quoted in CCC no. 163.

12 cf. St. Thérèse of Lisieux, *Story of a Soul,* I.C.S. Publications, 1976. p. 112.

13 *Story of a Soul*, p. 268 (emphasis added).

14 Vladimir Lossky, *Orthodox Theology*, St. Vladimir's Seminary Press, 1989, p. 91.

15 ibid., p.128.

16 St. Maximus the Confessor in Kallistos Ware, *The Orthodox Way*, Penguin Books, 1962, p. 236.

17 As my brother, Fr. J.A. Ihnatowicz of the University of St. Thomas in Houston, pointed out to me, there is, apparently, no mention of the two "selves" in Christian literature at least until the eighth century. Christian Fathers talked rather about "the old Adam" (the fallen man) and the "New Adam" (Christ and those who had been united to him). They also talked of "life of the flesh" and "life of the spirit." In both cases, as St. Augustine made quite clear, the whole human person was meant: body, soul and spirit. It meant the whole life of a person lived either still under the domination of sin,

or already "dead to sin" and restored by grace to the state God had created it to be.

18 Julian of Norwich, *Revelations of the Divine Love,* chapter 32.

19 See the Liturgy of St. John Chrysostom.

20 One of Catherine Doherty's favourite sayings was, "Man is cruciform: with one arm he reaches out to God, but woe to him if he does not embrace [his neighbour] with the other!" She often described herself as "a woman in love with God," and called all of us "to preach the Gospel with our lives."

21 Metropolitan Anthony Bloom once said that he liked to think that the original Greek word for mercy, *eleos,* was similar to the word for olive oil which, in ancient times, was used as healing ointment for wounds. He thought that this derivation, however "unscientific" it might be, expressed very well the true meaning of mercy. In a more "scientific" way, my brother pointed out that *eleos* could be translated as "compassionate love." It means a kind of love a stronger person has for a weaker one: a free offering of something which one cannot buy or deserve or capture by oneself. It might also be interesting to note that in Slavonic languages the expression "to have mercy" can be translated as "to be moved by love." Thus, in Polish, when we say, "Lord, have mercy!" we actually say, "Lord, please love me!"

22 see CCC no. 1730.

23 Lossky, op.cit., p. 80.

24 Mother Maria Gysi, *Letters,* p. 30.

25 *Catechism of the Catholic Church* no. 1030-32.

26 Ware, *The Orthodox Church*, Penguin Books, 1964, p. 260.

27 In some Catholic countries, local traditions survive that commemorate and celebrate the Tomb of Christ. There are also mentions of it in the Catholic liturgy of the hours (lauds, vespers and matins) prescribed for Holy Week, but these are mainly said by the clergy and few lay people; they are unknown to most Catholics. The public liturgies of Holy Week hardly mention it at all.

28 Ware, *The Orthodox Way*, p. 136.

Other books by Irma Zaleski

Living the Jesus Prayer

An ancient devotion in the Eastern Church, the Jesus Prayer is now becoming more familiar to Christians in the West. This slender volume is the perfect introduction to this time-honoured meditative prayer.

- 56 pages
- paperback
- ISBN 2-89088-792-8

The Way of Repentance

Drawing again on Eastern Christian tradition, Zaleski invites us to deeper knowledge of God's infinite forgiveness and mercy, taking a way largely neglected and obscured in the West.

This is the way of repentance: a constant attitude of heart, going beyond regret to healing, from guilt to liberation.

- 64 pages
- paperback
- ISBN 2-89088-980-7

Other books by Irma Zaleski

Mother Macrina

Using the fictitious character of Mother
Macrina, Zaleski has created stories of a modern
desert mother, resonant with the Eastern monastic
tradition. The thoughtful prose is complemented by
evocative woodcut illustrations.

- 96 pages
- paperback
- ISBN 2-89507-042-3